STARTING DESIGN & TECHNOLOGY

COMPUTER CONTROL

HENRY HAWES AND DAVID PARRY

Series editor: John Cave

CASSELL

Cassell Publishers Limited
Artillery House
Artillery Row
London SW1P 1RT

First published 1989

ISBN 0-304-31644-X

Typeset by Flairplan Typesetting Ltd., Ware, Herts.

Printed and bound in Great Britain by the Bath Press, Avon

CONTENTS

Introduction	5
Introducing the Computer	8
The BBC Computer	10
Getting Started	13
Keyboarding Skills	14
Programming	15
Programming Techniques	17
Control of the Screen	20
Modes	22
Discs	25
Movement on the Screen	27
Advanced Programming	30
External Control	34
Binary Numbers	35
Interfaces	37
Motors	45
Commercial Interfaces	46
Industrial Control	51
Technology and Computer Control	52
Mini-Dictionary	59
Index	62

Introduction

Any machine that works with numbers can be described as a computer. A calculator is a type of computer, and so is a slide rule.

This book is about working with computers. When you come across an important word for the first time, it will be printed in **bold**. Try to remember these words and what they mean.

Project 1

The earliest computers were mechanical. This computer has been designed to help count the mice, but it does not look as though it will work. Design a computer that you think will do better.

One of the earliest computers is the abacus.

Fact File

- Did you know that the abacus is still used today?

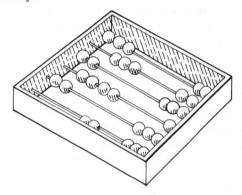

- Some people can work out calculations on an abacus faster than you could on an electronic calculator.

Introduction

- Did you know that the first electronic computers could carry out 1,000 calculations per second?
- The computers of tomorrow may work using light or super-conductors. They will be a million times faster – 1,000,000,000 calculations per second!
- During the Second World War, the computer used to break the German codes was called the Colossus. It was the size of a sports hall and used the same amount of electricity as a small town.
- The BBC computer of today has the power to do more complex tasks than Colossus.

This has allowed computers to be made smaller and more cheaply than ever before.
Today's business people can carry a complete computer around in their brief-case.

Even with all of these advances, the computer still works using a system of mathematics invented over 300 years ago:

BINARY

```
0  1  1  0  0  0  1  1
1  1  0  1  1  1  1  0
1  0  0  1  0  0  1  0
```

The computer has developed into a powerful tool for the designer. It can now be used as a word processor or as an aid for drawing (either with graphics or with **CAD** – Computer Aided Design).
The computer can also be used to **control** things. Control means putting the computer in charge of things. For example, industrial robots are controlled by computer to carry out tasks that humans would find difficult or dangerous.

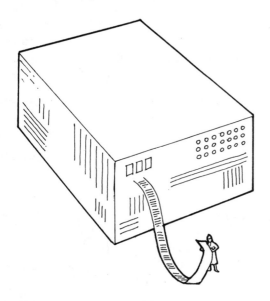

Modern computers use electronics and microelectronics to perform calculations on numbers.

- Make a list of tasks that computer-controlled robots are used for.
- Where else are computers used to control things?
- Choose one of the robots on your list and draw it in action.

Many people use BBC/ACORN computers, so throughout the rest of this book we shall be looking at ways of using this computer for control.

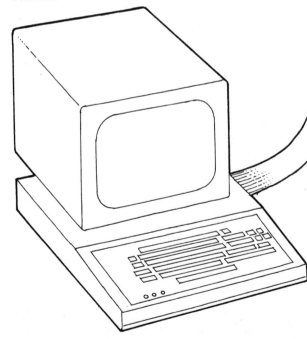

Some of the BBC/ACORN computers that you can use for control are:
  B
  B+
  Master
  Archimedes.

With some models, you may be able to try only some of the exercises in this book.

Introducing the Computer

All modern electronic computers are made from the same parts.

The five parts seen in all computers are:
1. Control unit
2. Storage unit
3. Arithmetic unit
4. Input
5. Output

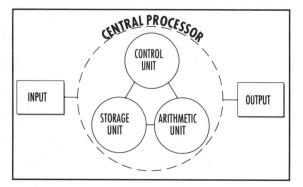

The control unit decides the order of work, what is involved and what end-product is required.

The storage unit is where information is held until it is needed. This memory is changed constantly as the computer is used.

The arithmetic unit carries out all of the calculations.

These three parts go together to form the central processing unit (**CPU**).

Input This is how information is fed into the computer. This can be done in many ways, such as from a keyboard.

Output This is how information is taken from the computer. Again this can be done in many ways, for example, the visual display unit (**VDU**), or screen, is one form of output.

A backing store is also found in many computers. This is another storage unit where extra information can be held for long periods of time. The backing store comes in many forms but you are most likely to see it as floppy discs or cassettes.

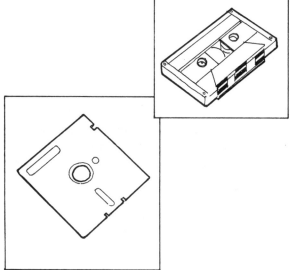

The elements of the computer work in the following way:

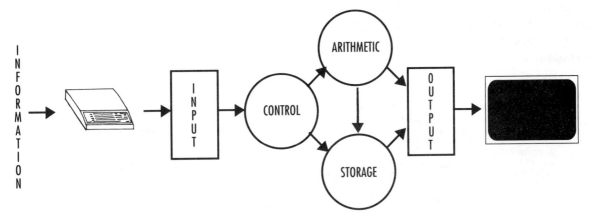

The first stage in using a computer is to give it some information – to input. This goes to the control unit which decides what to do. It chooses to send it to either the arithmetic unit or the storage unit. If it goes to the storage unit, it is held for later use. If it goes to the arithmetic unit, calculations are done. The results may then be sent to the storage unit or to the output.

Project 3

The path along which information has to travel through a computer is like a maze of wires.

On a sheet of A4 paper, design a maze which contains the five parts of the computer. These should be joined by the paths that the information could travel, plus lots of false routes.

Give your maze to a friend and see how quickly he or she can get through, going to each of the elements in turn.

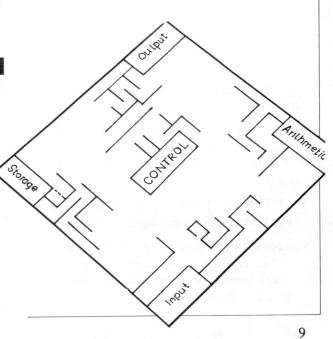

The BBC Computer

The Keyboard

When you work with computers, and in particular when you work with the BBC computer, most of the information that you input will be sent to the computer using the **keyboard**.

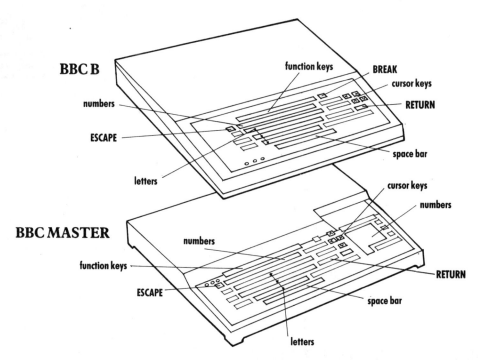

The important keys that you are going to use are:

Letters/numbers The computer understands a special language, called **BASIC**. You talk to the computer in this language using these keys.

RETURN This lets the computer know when you have finished a message.

Cursor keys The cursor is the flashing dot on the screen. It shows you where you are. These keys allow you to move the cursor around the screen.

BREAK This is like an on/off button. If you touch it, the computer will forget everything that you have told it. DON'T TOUCH IT!

ESCAPE This key is a bit like the BREAK key: it stops whatever the computer is doing, but the computer should not forget the instructions it has been given.

Function keys These are coloured red and are used for special tasks.

The Central Processor Unit

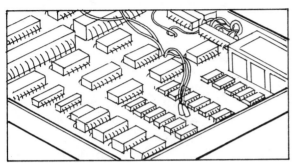

Underneath the keyboard, inside the case, are all of the electronics that make up the central processor unit. The CPU works on the information that you have sent to the computer from the keyboard. It then sends out other information from holes into which wires go. These holes are called **ports**. They are used to connect the computer to its outside devices.

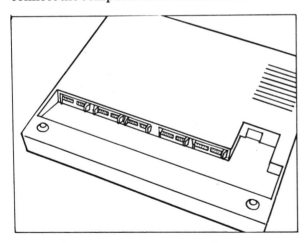

These devices are known as **peripherals**. The ones that you will see are:

The VDU

The Visual Display Unit is the screen on which you see information etc. It is an output device.

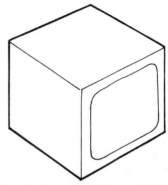

The Disc-Drive or Cassette Player

This is a storage device used for holding extra information, rather like a book. It can be an input or output device.

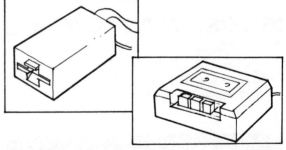

The Printer

This is an output device that is used to give you a printed copy of some of the work being done by the computer.

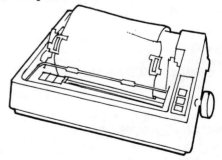

The BBC Computer

Project 4

Name the five parts of a computer shown in this diagram.

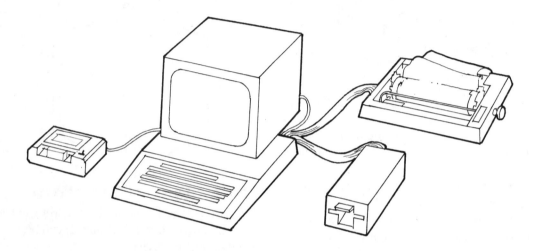

Fact File

- Computers are being developed that can understand the human voice. Soon we may be able to input information to a computer just by talking to it.

Project 5

Draw a table which shows the following devices as:

Central processor
Keyboard
Disc-drive
Printer
VDU
Memory
Plotter
Robot arm

INPUT	CPU	OUTPUT

Computers, and all of the bits that go with them, can be easily damaged. So it is important that everything is connected properly before you switch on. Ask your teacher to check that the computer is connected to the VDU and to the disc-drive (or cassette recorder). If it is not, you can check the connections (with your teacher) using this diagram.

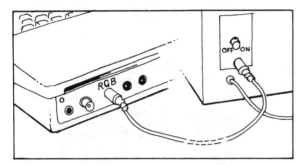

Once you are sure that everything is connected correctly, you can start. First plug the computer and VDU into the mains (some disc-drives need to be connected to the mains as well).

Be careful – mains voltages are dangerous.

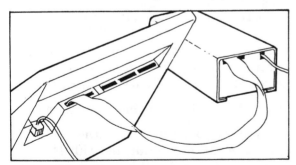

Now you can switch on. There is a black on/off switch on the back of the computer – turn this on. The computer should 'beep' and a red light (marked – caps locked) will come on. There will also be an on/off switch on the VDU. Ask your teacher where this is, and switch it on. The screen should light up.

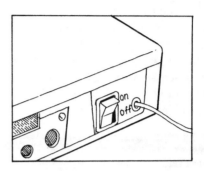

A message should appear in the top left-hand corner of the VDU screen. It will read something like

```
BBC Computer 32K
BASIC
> -
```

Finally, if there is a switch on the disc-drive, switch that on.

If you have any problems, ask your teacher for help. Do not try to fix anything yourself!

Now you should be ready to start.

Keyboarding Skills

Earlier we looked at what the parts of the computer do; now it's time to try using them. *Remember:* When you press a key, you are inputing information to the computer. The computer processes it in the CPU, and outputs to the VDU for you to see. So, sit in front of the keyboard and let's start.

1 Touch a key – you do not have to press hard. What happens?

2 Now hold a key down. What happens this time?

3 Type your name. Now press the **RETURN** key. (From now on we will use ‹RTN› to show when you should press the return key.) What happened?

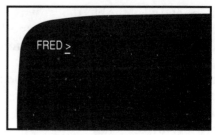

FRED ›

4 Try typing PRINT and then your name, then press ‹RTN›. Remember to record what happens.

5 Try that again, but this time put " before and after your name, for example:

PRINT "FRED"

(The " is above the number 2. To get it you need to hold down the SHIFT key and press the 2.)
What did the computer do this time?

In fact what you have done is tell the computer to print your name on the screen. When you pressed ‹RTN› it carried out your instruction.

Your first piece of programming – well done!

Until you sent your instructions to the computer in the correct order and with the correct letters, spaces and dots, etc. it could not carry out your instructions. That is why you got funny messages on the screen.

6 A useful instruction to try now is:
CLS‹RTN›
Watch what happens.

Programming

As you work through the rest of this book you will learn more instructions for the computer. This will help you to write programs to make the computer carry out more difficult tasks. It will help if you keep a careful record of what instructions do and how to use them. So start making a list of instructions on your note pad.

As we saw earlier, the computer will only understand your instructions if you send them in a certain way. It only understands a certain language, just as you understand English. If a foreign word appears, it does not make sense. So you must be careful to use the computer's language when you give it instructions.

Fact File

- The BBC computer understands a language called BASIC. This stands for Beginner's All-purpose Symbolic Instruction Code.

A series of instructions put together for the computer is called a **program**. The computer will carry out the instructions in a set order. The order is set by giving each line of instructions a number: for example, 1 PRINT"FRED".

The computer will always start with the lowest line number. It will then carry on through 2, 3 4, etc. unless you tell it to change the order. Try the following:

What happened?
In a program with line numbers, the computer will not start until you tell it to. You do this with the instruction RUN ‹RTN›.
Try typing that now.

What happens?

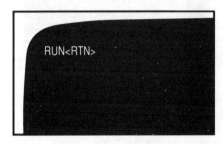

What happens if you type RUN ‹RTN› again?

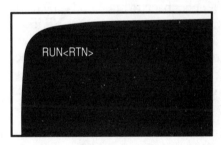

The computer has remembered your program and will repeat it every time you instruct it to do so.

Programming

This time we will try a longer program.

```
1 PRINT"FRED"
2 GOTO 1
3 END
```

Run this program and see what happens. Did it work? A column of FRED should have appeared. To stop it, press ESCAPE.
Let's look and see what was happening.
You should know that PRINT"FRED" tells the computer to write the word FRED on the screen. The second line, 2, says GOTO 1, so the computer goes back to line 1 and repeats that instruction. The computer writes FRED on the screen again. Then it goes to line 2 again, where it is told to go back to line 1 again. So it keeps on writing FRED on the screen.
This is called a **loop**, because the computer loops back to an earlier line.

In this program the computer can never reach line 3, which would have told the computer that it had reached the END of the programe.

The **ESCAPE** key that you pressed allowed you to escape from the program, otherwise it would have gone on for ever. This is one of the times when the escape key is useful, as it can get you out of a program without losing the program from the computer's memory.

If you had pressed BREAK instead, your program would have been lost for ever from the computer's memory. Although it is best to type program lines in the correct order, there are times when this cannot be done – for instance, when you need to add extra lines. In cases like this the computer will put the lines in the correct order for you.

Try typing

```
5 END
2 PRINT"FRED"
3 PRINT" "
1 CLS
4 GOTO2
```

and RUN ‹RTN› the program.

Did it work?
You should have a column of FRED moving up the screen.
Press ESCAPE to stop the program.
The computer must have put the lines of the program into the correct order for it to work.
You can check this by 'listing' your program on the screen. To do this type in

```
LIST <RTN>
```

The program should come up on the screen with the lines in the correct order.
Add this instruction to your note pad.

Project 6

Write a sentence to explain the meaning of each of these words/instructions:

Program	Loop	GOTO	RUN	Escape
Basic	PRINT	<RTN>	LIST	Break

Programming Techniques

As we saw earlier, a program is a series of instructions or commands which are put together in a certain order to make the computer do things. Computers are not the only things that can be controlled by a program. You can be, too. We will look at how programs work in this section.

Before starting to write a program for a computer, there are certain things that you must do:

1 You must decide exactly what the aim of the program is.
2 List what you want the program to do in a **flow chart**. This will help you to make sure the commands are in the correct order.
3 Write out what you want the computer to do at each stage.
4 Try a **dry run**. Work through the program in your head or on paper before putting it on to the computer.

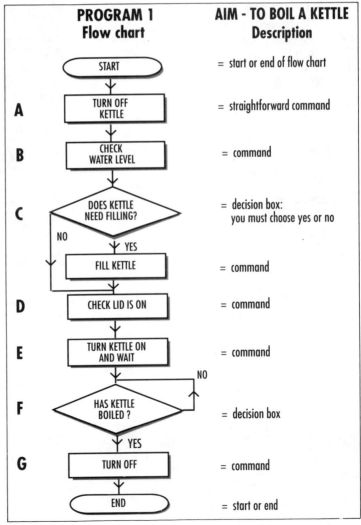

PROGRAM 1 Flow chart	AIM - TO BOIL A KETTLE Description
START	= start or end of flow chart
A TURN OFF KETTLE	= straightforward command
B CHECK WATER LEVEL	= command
C DOES KETTLE NEED FILLING?	= decision box: you must choose yes or no
FILL KETTLE	= command
D CHECK LID IS ON	= command
E TURN KETTLE ON AND WAIT	= command
F HAS KETTLE BOILED?	= decision box
G TURN OFF	= command
END	= start or end

Let's try writing a program. This program is not for a computer; it is for you to boil a kettle.

Programming Techniques

We have got the aim of the program and drawn a flow chart. Now we must explain what should happen at each stage.

       START

A = The kettle is turned off for safety. This is a straightforward command.

B = The water-level must be checked – a straightforward command.

C = This could be called a PROCEDURE. If the kettle needs water, *then* carry out the procedure. If it does not, *then* do not carry out the procedure. Procedure = Fill up kettle.

D = Straightforward command.

E = Straightforward command.

F = This is a controlled loop. Repeat checking to see if it has boiled UNTIL it has boiled.

G = Straightforward command.

      END

After the dry run everything appears to be all right, so here is the 'program'.

```
10   REM how to boil a kettle
20   turn off kettle
30   check water level
40   PROCfillup

50   check lid
60   turn on
70   REPEAT

80   has it boiled?
90   UNTIL it has boiled
100  turn it off
110  END




120  DEF PROCfillup


130  IF kettle does not
         need water
         THEN GOTO line 50
140  add water
150  GOTO line 130
160  ENDPROC
```

REM means REMark.

PROCfillup is an abbreviation for PROCedure fill up kettle.

REPEAT....UNTIL carries out a routine untill certain conditions are met.

END is the END of the program, but some statements can come after this.

DEFinition of the PROCedure fillup kettle.

IF the kettle is all right, THEN lines 140, 150, 160 will be ignored.

END of PROCedure.

Note: This program will not run on the BBC but it is a program and it does contain some of the commands used by the BBC.

Project 7

Using the methods we have outlined, write a program for one of the following:
- making a cup of tea/coffee
- crossing the road
- doing up a shoe-lace
- the journey home from school

We have tried to write a program that you can follow; now let's try one for the computer.

| **PROGRAM 2** | **AIM - MULTIPLY** |
| **Flow chart** | **TWO NUMBERS** |

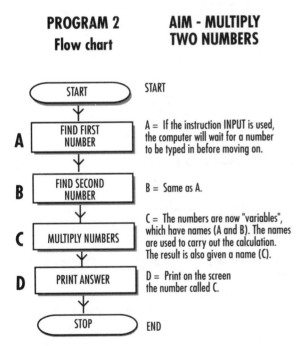

START — START

A — FIND FIRST NUMBER — A = If the instruction INPUT is used, the computer will wait for a number to be typed in before moving on.

B — FIND SECOND NUMBER — B = Same as A.

C — MULTIPLY NUMBERS — C = The numbers are now "variables", which have names (A and B). The names are used to carry out the calculation. The result is also given a name (C).

D — PRINT ANSWER — D = Print on the screen the number called C.

STOP — END

Dry run appears all right, so here is the program:

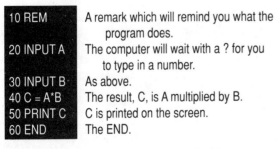

10 REM	A remark which will remind you what the program does.
20 INPUT A	The computer will wait with a ? for you to type in a number.
30 INPUT B	As above.
40 C = A*B	The result, C, is A multiplied by B.
50 PRINT C	C is printed on the screen.
60 END	The END.

This program will work on the BBC, so try it.

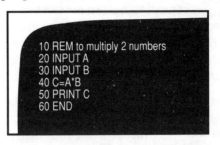

```
10 REM to multiply 2 numbers
20 INPUT A
30 INPUT B
40 C=A*B
50 PRINT C
60 END
```

Don't forget to type

```
RUN<RTN>
```

Project 8

Try writing programs to carry out other calculations.

Fact File

- Try multiplying 7,686,369,774,870 × 2,465,099,745,799 in your head.
  Mrs Shakuntala Devi from India came up with the correct answer of 18,947,668,177,995,426,462,773,730 in 28 seconds!

19

Control of the Screen

The aim of this book is to help you to make the computer control things. In the last few chapters we have learnt a number of useful instructions and techniques, but we have not yet written a control program. Now you will have that chance.

One area that can be controlled is the screen. The screen, or VDU, can be used for many things other than just printing your name. It can be used for showing information in graphs, as pictures, or as a mix of pictures and writing.

One window, same size as screen

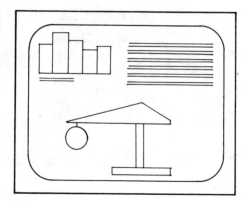

Three windows, different sizes and shapes

The screen can be thought of as a 'window'. You can look into the window and see what the computer is doing. You can change the size of the window and you can also look into more than one window at a time.

We are going to learn how to control windows; in other words, make them do what we want them to do.

The first thing to remember is that there are two types of window:

1 Text – writing will appear in this window.
2 Graphics – pictures can be put into this window.

The two types of window are given different code-names by the computer. When you type in VDU it tells the computer that a code number is coming.

VDU 24 is the code for a graphics window. VDU 28 is the code for a text window.

These codes tell the computer that something is to be done to the window, and the first thing to be done is to say where the window should be on the screen and how big it should be. For this you use co-ordinates. A co-ordinate is a pair of numbers that gives the position of any point on the screen. One gives the distance across the screen, the other the distance up the screen.

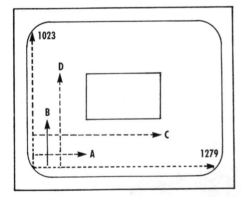

Let's look at just the graphics window. For graphics, the screen is said to be 1,279 units long and 1,023 units high. This is numbered from the bottom left-hand corner. To position a graphics window, you need four co-ordinates. These are put after the VDU 24 command: for example, VDU 24,A;B;C;D;

VDU 24,100;100;1000;800; will give a graphics window of 900 units long by 700 units tall, and positioned 100 units across the screen and 100 units up the screen.

Note: Make sure all of the , and ; are put in the correct places.

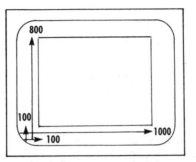

VDU 24,100;100;1000;800;

Project 9

Work out the VDU code to put a small graphics window in the centre of the screen. Say how big (in mm) you think it would be.
Now work out a second VDU code to put a graphics window in the top right-hand corner of the screen. This window should cover about a quarter of the screen.

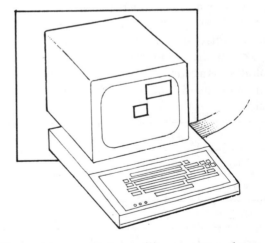

These commands alone will appear to make little or no difference to the screen, but if they are put into a short program, some interesting effects can be achieved. One of these effects is to use colour. Both types of window can be coloured in, but more codes are needed.

21

Modes

The computer has several different ways of working when you want to put windows on to the screen. These are called **modes**.
When the computer is switched on it is normally used for writing programs. So you only need black and white. This is Mode 7. Just black and white is not very interesting, we want more colours. So we will use Mode 2, which will give us the choice of 16 colours. Hence, at the beginning of each program we write that will contain windows, we will tell the computer to work in Mode 2.

Although we will now have 16 colours to use, it will be simplest to explain how to use just 4 of them: black, red, green, yellow.

For the moment, let us deal with just the graphic background colours – that is the colour of the screen itself, not the colour of what is on it.

As the screen is normally black with white writing (text), we will not try to colour a window black as it will be invisible, but we can work with the other three colours. Each of these colours has a code-number which the computer will understand. The codes are in the table below.

	FOREGROUND	BACKGROUND
BLACK	0	128
RED	1	129
GREEN	2	130
YELLOW	3	131

A final command that you need is GCOL, which tells the computer what colour is to be used for a certain operation. For instance, GCOL 0,129 will colour the screen or window red. The 0 tells the computer to use the colour 129 (red) to colour in a certain area (in this case the window).

Project 10

Make a list of all the commands that are needed when you want to put coloured windows on to the screen and explain what they do.

So far the window is still invisible, so a trick, which will show the colour of the window, is to clear the screen. This wipes the screen and returns it to the background colour – but, you have changed the background colour!

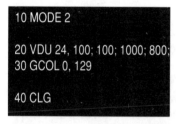

10 MODE 2	Tells the computer to use Mode 2.
20 VDU 24, 100; 100; 1000; 800;	Sets a window.
30 GCOL 0, 129	Sets background colour to red.
40 CLG	Abbreviation of Clear Graphics window.

Try this program and see what happens.

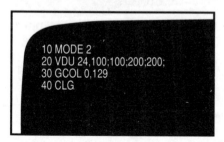

```
10 MODE 2
20 VDU 24,100;100;200;200;
30 GCOL 0,129
40 CLG
```

Note: If nothing happens, check that you haven't left out a ; or a ,.
Try to move the window around the screen. Keep a record of what you do.

Try changing the colour of the window. Keep a record of what you do.
What about two windows? Try adding:

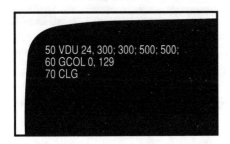

```
50 VDU 24, 300; 300; 500; 500;
60 GCOL 0, 129
70 CLG
```

What happens?

See if you can build up three windows, then four.

Now try to build up two windows of different colours.

Note: Remember black windows are invisible.

If you think that you can get graphics windows to go where you want, then try this project. Write a program that uses graphics windows to draw a picture of a face. Remember to use the methods for programming that we learnt earlier.

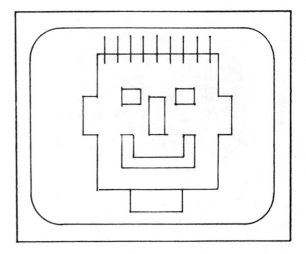

Modes

Another interesting thing that you can do with graphics windows is to change their colour. This means that you can produce a sequence of colours in the same window.

You can do this simply by adding more GCOL commands.

Try:

```
10 MODE2
20 VDU 24, 100; 100; 1000; 800;
30 GCOL 0, 129
40 CLG
50 GCOL 0, 130
60 CLG
70 GCOL 0, 131
80 CLG
90 END
```

Watch what happens.

The graphics window changes colour, but it does it very quickly. With this program you do not have any control over what is happening. What we need is for the computer to wait for a little while between colour changes. This will need a new command.

W=INKEY(100)

We can think of this as telling the computer to wait for 100 hundredths of a second (that is 1 second). You can, of course, change the number to make the computer wait for a longer (or shorter) time.

Let's try a new program:

```
10 MODE2
20 VDU 24, 100; 100; 1000; 800;
30 GCOL 0, 129
40 CLG
50 W=INKEY (600)
60 GCOL 0, 131
70 CLG
80 END
```

Run this and watch what happens.

Now run the program again. After two or three seconds, press any key. What happens?

In fact the command allows you to override the time delay. This will make it quite a useful command.

Project 12

By now you should know quite a lot about controlling graphics windows on the screen. You should also have a program to draw a face on the screen. What I want you to do now is try to improve that program to make your face's eyes and mouth open and close.

If you get that to work, how about writing programs to make disco lights on the screen, or design some traffic-lights?

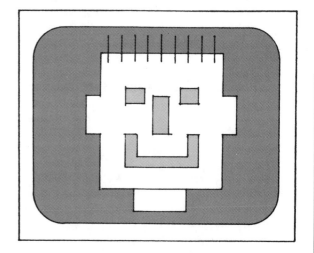

24

Discs

By now a lot of programs that you are writing are taking a long time to input to the computer by typing. It is a shame to lose them each time the computer is switched off. This is why backing stores are made for computers.

It is quite likely that you have a disc-drive connected to the computer. The backing store is the **disc** that you put into the drive unit.

The disc is a piece of magnetic material, like a big piece of cassette tape, inside a protective case.

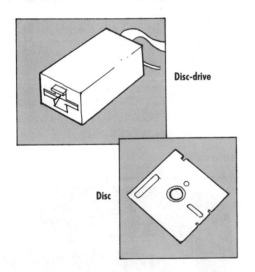

Disc-drive

Disc

Note: Never touch the magnetic material or you might damage it and the information stored on it may be lost.

The disc spins inside the disc-drive, rather like an LP on a record-player. To work properly, the disc must have 'tracks' on it, like the grooves on an LP. These are put on when you **format** the disc.

Information can then be **saved** on these tracks. Later it can be **loaded** back into the computer.

Let's try saving a program.
First, you will need to get a disc that has been formatted, and put it into the disc-drive. If you are not sure about this, then ask your teacher.
Type a short program:

```
10 PRINT"FRED"
20.GOTO10
30 END
```

To save this on disc you have to tell the computer to save it, and give the program a name, which should be no more than seven letters.
So let's try:

```
SAVE"FRED" <RTN>
```

The disc-drive should make a noise. When it stops, the program has been saved. This is called a **file**. To check that it has been saved, you can look to see what is on the **catalogue** of the disc.

Project 13

We will look at a lot of commands for use with the backing store. Copy them onto your note pad and make sure that you write down how each command works and what it does.

Discs

Type:

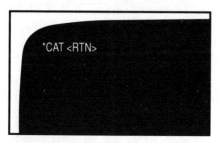

You should see some information and somewhere should be the name of your file. Take the disc out of the drive and switch off the computer.

Note: Always take the disc out before you switch anything off, or you might damage the disc.

Now switch on again, put the disc back in, and we will try to load the information back into the computer.
Type:

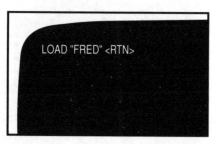

The disc should make a noise again. Now list or run the program to make sure it is there.

It is very easy to copy your program over someone else's if you use the same name. So always check what names have been used first. You can protect your files by **locking** them on to the disc. This needs a new command:

*ACCESS

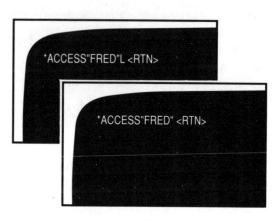

The L locks it. To unlock the file so that you can change it etc., you use the same command but without the L.

One final command is to **wipe** files off the disc when you have finished with them. We use the command ★WIPE because it double-checks that you want to get rid of the file.

After typing in:

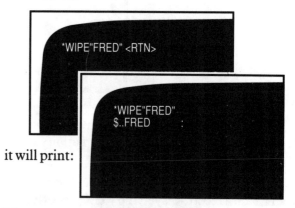

it will print:

If you want to wipe the file, type Y.
If you have made a mistake or changed your mind, then type N.

Check what you have done by looking on the catalogue.

Movement on the Screen

So far we have controlled colour and windows. Now let's try to control movement on the screen. To draw a picture, you use a sheet of paper and a pencil. On the computer we will use a graphics window and the cursor. You would normally make the pencil move with your hand, but now you will have to use the computer to control the cursor.

In a graphics window, the position of the cursor is given by two co-ordinates, X,Y. The co-ordinates always start with 0,0 in the bottom left-hand corner of the window. Each time you give the computer a new set of co-ordinates, the computer will DRAW a line from the old cursor position to the new cursor position.

Let's look at a program:

10 MODE 2	Put the computer into a graphics mode.
20 VDU 24, 10; 10; 1200; 1000;	Set up a large graphics window.
30 GCOL 0, 129	Put the window into a colour.
40 CLG	Make the window visible.
50 DRAW 500, 500	Computer draws a line from the first cursor position (the origin 0,0) to position 500.
60 DRAW 500, 600	
70 DRAW 600, 600	Instructions to draw a square in the middle of the window.
80 DRAW 600, 500	
90 DRAW 500, 500	
100 END	End of program.

Run this program. You should get:

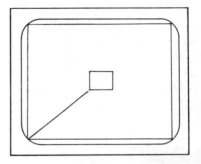

Project 14

Try drawing some more shapes in the window, like these ones.

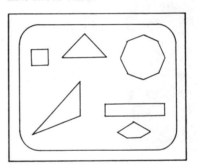

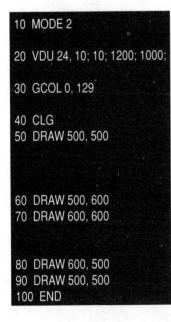

27

Movement on the Screen

You should by now have written programs to draw several different shapes. The trouble is that each shape will be joined to the last shape. This is because the DRAW command will always leave a line as the cursor goes from one position to another. To draw more difficult pictures we need to be able to MOVE the cursor without drawing a line.

Try this program:

10 MODE 2	Put computer in graphics mode.
20 VDU 24, 10; 10; 1200; 1000;	Set up a graphics window.
30 GCOL 0, 129	Put window into colour.
40 CLG	Make window visible.
50 MOVE 400, 400	Move cursor from origin to 400, 400.
60 DRAW 600, 600	Draw line.
70 MOVE 600, 500	Move cursor.
80 DRAW 400, 300	Draw line.
90 END	End program.

Run this program and record what happens.

Project 15

If this program works OK, then experiment with the two commands DRAW and MOVE. Draw some more shapes, then develop them to make a pattern for a snowflake.

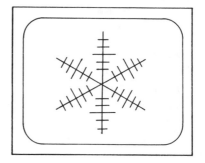

Now try to program the computer to draw a hi-fi unit.

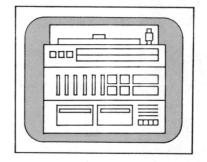

We mentioned earlier in the book that it is possible to change the background colour of a graphics window using a GCOL 0, command. The same command can be used to change the foreground colour, that is, the colour that is used for drawing. This means that you can get even more interesting effects. As with the background colours, the foreground colours are given numbers.

Here is a table of all the colours that you can use in Mode 2, with their background and foreground numbers.

PLAIN COLOURS	FOREGROUND	BACKGROUND
Black	0	128
Red	1	129
Green	2	130
Yellow	3	131
Blue	4	132
Magenta	5	133
Cyan	6	134
White	7	135
FLASHING COLOURS		
White/Black	8	136
Red/Cyan	9	137
Green/Magenta	10	138
Yellow/Blue	11	139
Blue/Yellow	12	140
Magenta/Green	13	141
Cyan/Red	14	142
Black/White	15	143

Try this program with its different colours. Then make up some more of your own.

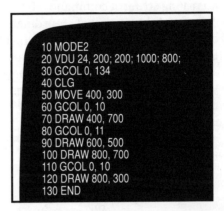

```
10 MODE2
20 VDU 24, 200; 200; 1000; 800;
30 GCOL 0, 134
40 CLG
50 MOVE 400, 300
60 GCOL 0, 10
70 DRAW 400, 700
80 GCOL 0, 11
90 DRAW 600, 500
100 DRAW 800, 700
110 GCOL 0, 10
120 DRAW 800, 300
130 END
```

Fact File

- The world's most powerful and fastest computer is the Cray-2. It has 32 million bytes of main memory and can do 250 million operations per second!

Advanced Programming

The programs that we have written for the control of drawing on the screen must be written as a long string of commands. It would be much easier if the next set of co-ordinates could be **INPUT** after each line is drawn. This requires new commands. The programs are also a bit more complicated. But do not be put off. If you follow the methods of programming that we used earlier in the book, it should all be quite easy.

The aim of the program:
- Set up a graphics window
- Decide to move or draw
- Give computer some co-ordinates
- Move or draw line
- Repeat

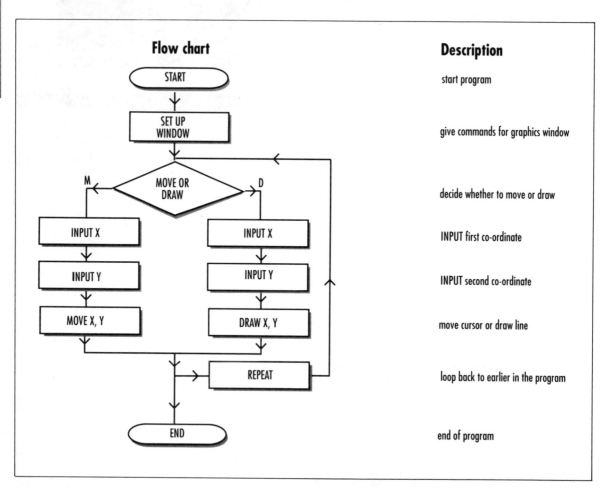

Flow chart	Description
START	start program
SET UP WINDOW	give commands for graphics window
MOVE OR DRAW	decide whether to move or draw
INPUT X	INPUT first co-ordinate
INPUT Y	INPUT second co-ordinate
MOVE X, Y / DRAW X, Y	move cursor or draw line
REPEAT	loop back to earlier in the program
END	end of program

Sounds OK. But what about the program itself?

The first part we have seen before,

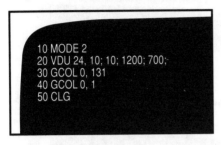

```
10 MODE 2
20 VDU 24, 10; 10; 1200; 700;
30 GCOL 0, 131
40 GCOL 0, 1
50 CLG
```

but the rest is new. So note down the new commands and what they do.

Note: We have used these line numbers to make it easier to see the different parts of the program.

100 INPUT "M OR D" A$	INPUT some information (to the computer). We will call this information A$. The $ tells the computer to expect a letter not a number.
110 IF A$="M" GOTO 300	If the letter that has been input is M, then the computer jumps to line 300.
200 INPUT "X" X	Print "X" on the screen, and INPUT a co-ordinate X.
210 INPUT "Y" Y	Print "Y" on the screen, and INPUT a co-ordinate Y.
220 DRAW X, Y	Draw a line from old cursor position to new co-ordinates.
230 GOTO 100	Return to line 100 in the program.
300 INPUT "X" XX	INPUT co-ordinate X to computer. The program has XX so that it is not confused with X.
310 INPUT "Y" YY	INPUT co-ordinate Y to computer. The program has YY so that it is not confused with Y.
320 MOVE XX, YY	Move to new cursor position.
330 GOTO 100	Return to line 100 in the program.
400 END	End of program.

Advanced Programming

The dry run looks good. Let's type it into the computer and see if it works. Fingers crossed!

You should first see:

The computer is asking you to input either M for move or D for draw.

Type in:

Next on the screen should be:

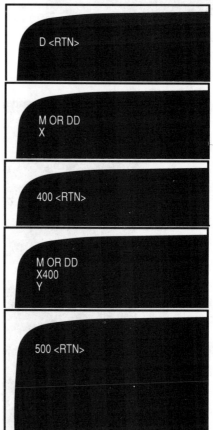

so type in an X co-ordinate:

Then you should see:

so type in a Y co-ordinate:

The computer, hopefully, will draw a line to your co-ordinates. Then it will ask you M or D again.

Experiment with this program some more. Try moving as well as drawing.

You may well have found out that the instructions you input to the computer soon start covering the graphics window. Obviously this ruins your drawing.
What can we do about it?

Remember back to text windows? Well, this is where we will try to use one.
We need to set up a VDU command for a text window so that all of the writing stays within the space on the screen. Graphics windows need co-ordinates; so do text windows. But this time the numbers are different.

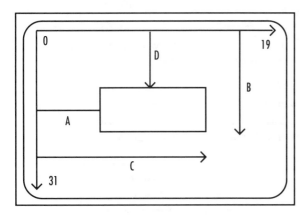

For this program we will use:
VDU 28,2,10,10,5,
but we could have used other numbers.

Note: This VDU command uses , in all places, not ;.
So add this line to your program

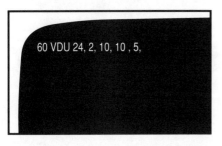

60 VDU 24, 2, 10, 10 , 5,

and try the program again.

Does it help?

Now save the program on to disc.

Project 16

Remember the maze that you designed in Project 3? Redraw it on to tracing paper so that it fits over the graphics window in this program. Now carefully tape it on the screen. Using the program we have just written, see if you can use the cursor to draw a path through your maze.
Let a friend have a go. See who can get through giving the computer the least number of move or draw instructions.

If you are feeling confident, how about trying to change the program so that you can change the colour of the line as the program is running?

Fact File

- The world's smallest word processor is the Easi-Text 1350. It is based on a computer that measures only $182 \times 72 \times 16$ mm. Together with its printer, it can easily fit into a brief-case.

External Control

Throughout this book the aim has been to let you control things using the computer. Let's now look at how to control things that you have designed and made, such as buggies, turtles or robots. These are all external to the computer, so they will need **external control**.

Anything that you want to control outside the computer will have to be plugged into the computer somewhere. How else is the computer going to control it? The computer has several holes into which things can be plugged.

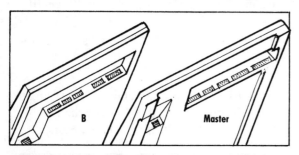

The correct name for these holes (or sockets) is **port**. Each port is used for a special job, such as the disc-drive or the printer. We will use just one of the ports, the **user port**.

This socket, or port, allows information in the form of electrical signals to pass in or out of the computer. For the moment we are only going to use it to send information out.

The computer responds to a range of code-numbers which tell the computer which ports to switch on or off.

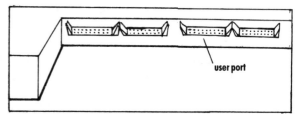

user port

The code ?65122 = 255 will first tell the computer to **OUTPUT** through the user port.

The user port has 20 possible connections, 8 of which are useful for output. For you to be able to switch these 8 on and off, you need to be able to use the binary (base 2) number system.

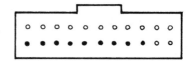

Binary Numbers

Computers are not very clever. They run on electricity and can only understand when it is on or off. For a computer, 0 means off and 1 means on. 0s and 1s are the basic ingredients of the binary numbers which computers always use.

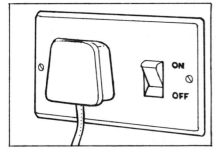

The numbers that we normally use are in decimal (base 10). Each number is 10 times bigger than the number in the column on its right.

decimal numbers: 1000s 100s 10s 1s

The binary, or base 2, system is similar, but each column is twice as big as the column to its right.

binary numbers: •
128s 64s 32s 16s 8s 4s 2s 1s

Let's look at a binary number,
10110101

To change it to a decimal number, you add the headings of all the columns where there is a 1. So,

128 64 32 16 8 4 2 1

1   0   1   1   0 1 0 1

$128 + 32 + 16 + 4 + 1 = 181$

As we have already discussed, there are eight usable connections in the user port. These are labelled.

PB7 PB6 PB5 PB4 PB3 PB2 PB1 PB0

128 64 32 16 8 4 2 1

and correspond to the column headings of the binary system.

When there is a 1 in a column, it means that the output line is switched on. So to turn the output lines on, you must add the column values together. This number then makes up part of the code that you give to the computer.

Fact File

- In the Mato Grosso of Brazil live the Nambiquara people. They aren't bothered by decimal or binary. They don't use a number system at all!

Binary Numbers

For example, if you want all eight lines on, you would add all the headings together.

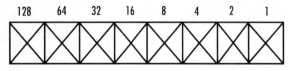

$$128 + 64 + 32 + 16 + 8 + 4 + 2 + 1 = 255$$

Then you would use the number 255 as part of the code.

If every other line were required, every other heading would be added:
$$128 + 32 + 8 + 2 = 170$$

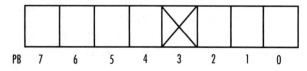

Just line four on:

$$8 = 8$$

The number by itself is not much use. It has to be used as part of a bigger code. We have already seen that ?65122 = 255 tells the computer to output through the user port. Well, a similar code tells the computer which switches, or **lines**, of the port to switch on. This code is

?65120 =

The number that you have worked out is then put into the code after the =.
So

?65120 = 255
would switch on all of the eight lines.

?65120 = 181
would switch on lines 7,5,4,2,0.

Change the following binary numbers into decimal numbers:
11001100
10101010
01010101
11000011

Now work out the code that will switch on output lines:
7,5,2,1
5,4,3,2
7,6,4,3,2,1
5,3,

Try a few more of your own.

Here are some more interesting facts about numbers.
- Did you know that a centillion is 1 followed by 600 noughts?
- The least exciting reading has got to be the Japanese print-out of the value of pi (π). It was 20,000 pages long and gave pi to 133,554,000 places.

Interfaces

Although the computer is plugged into the mains, it works on only 5 volts. There is a transformer inside it which reduces the voltage. Do not be fooled into thinking that 'only 5 volts' is not dangerous. IT IS!

WARNING
Do not plug anything into the computer until it has been checked by an expert!

We have seen that you only need two commands to be able to control things external to the computer. The trouble is that there is little spare power for the computer to drive external devices, such as bulbs or motors. So we will have to use an **interface**.

An interface is a box of tricks that goes between the computer and whatever is being controlled. It will normally have a power source of its own. So when the computer is used to switch it on, it is powerful enough to switch on the other devices, like motors.

an **integrated circuit** (a microchip) which keeps the current where it is needed.

To be able to try out our external control commands, we are going to need an interface. You can buy them, but they are expensive and they usually do a lot more than we need. So, with the help of a teacher, you could have a go at making a simple interface. This will allow you to switch on and off a series of LEDs (Light Emitting Diodes). These look like small bulbs. Making the interface will involve soldering together some electronic components. You will see how they fit together in Project 18.

Note

- Even a battery has the power to give you a very nasty shock. *Be careful with electricity.*

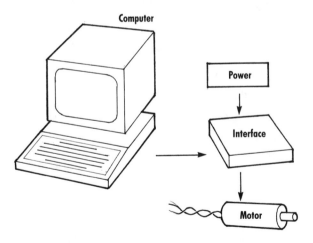

One important thing about interfaces is that they must not allow large currents to go back into the computer, otherwise the electronics inside the computer may be ruined. So the interface will contain a **buffer**. This is normally

Interfaces

You are going to make a simple interface by joining these parts together.

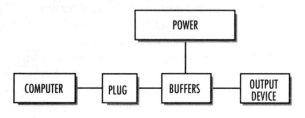

You will need a special plug to fit into the user port. This will be connected to the rest of the interface with wire. Then there are the buffers. You will need two integrated circuits, as each one can only deal with four lines. These will be powered by a small battery, which can be connected with a battery snap. The output devices will be eight LEDs. Each of these will need a protective resistor. Finally, you must remember to connect the 0v from the computer to the 0v of the battery. This is so they both are at the same starting level.

This is what your interface should look like.

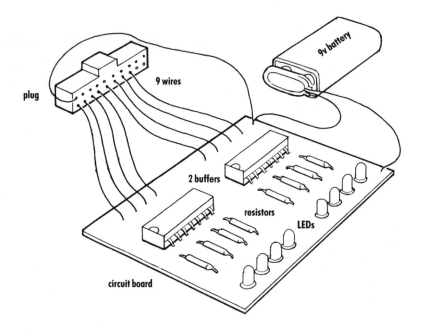

Here is the circuit diagram to show the connections:

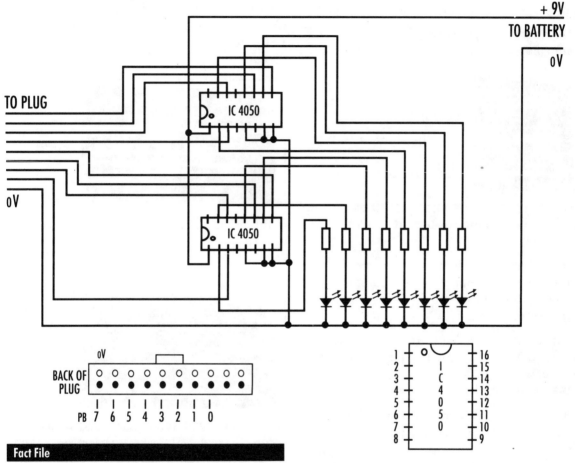

BACK OF PLUG

PB 7 6 5 4 3 2 1 0

```
1  ─┤○      ├─ 16
2  ─┤   I   ├─ 15
3  ─┤   C   ├─ 14
4  ─┤   4   ├─ 13
5  ─┤   0   ├─ 12
6  ─┤   5   ├─ 11
7  ─┤   0   ├─ 10
8  ─┤       ├─ 9
```

Fact File

- Integrated circuits, like the ones we are using, contain switches. They are very fast. These circuits could switch on or off about 3,000,000 times a second. That's fast! But there are integrated circuits that can switch on or off 100 times faster than that, 300,000,000 times a second.

The components that you will need are:
1 20-way plug
2 IC 4050
2 16-pin IC holders
8 1K2 resistors
8 LEDs
1 battery snap
1 piece of circuit board
some wire

Good luck, but be careful, and do not try the interface until it has been checked by a teacher.

39

Interfaces

Now you can try out some external control with your simple interface. Plug it into the user port.

Here is a short program using the two commands we looked at earlier. Try it out.

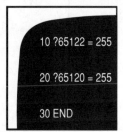

10 ?65122 = 255 — All user port lines set to output.

20 ?65120 = 255 — All output lines turned on.

30 END — End of program.

Try altering the code-number after the = in line 20. This should allow you to turn on or off different LEDs.

This, in principle, is how all devices are controlled by the computer – outputs are either on or off. LEDs are on or off, motors can be turned on or off, etc.

To make the program more useful, it can be adapted to make the value a **variable**. This is a number which can be altered either by the computer or the user.

Let's try letting the computer change the number, the variable. We will need to alter line 20.

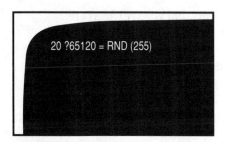

```
20 ?65120 = RND (255)
```

This will tell the computer to pick a number below 255 at RaNDom. So a random set of LEDs will switch on.

If we put a GOTO command in the program, the LEDs will be switched on and off at random, until you tell it to stop by pressing the ESCAPE key.
Try:

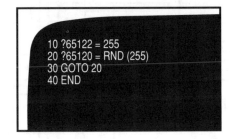

```
10 ?65122 = 255
20 ?65120 = RND (255)
30 GOTO 20
40 END
```

In this program, the LEDs only flash on and off.

If you add

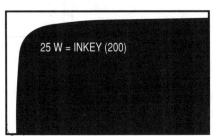

```
25 W = INKEY (200)
```

the computer will wait for 200 hundredths of a second (2 seconds) for a key to be pressed. If no key is pressed, it will carry on to the next line.

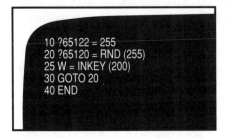

```
10 ?65122 = 255
20 ?65120 = RND (255)
25 W = INKEY (200)
30 GOTO 20
40 END
```

What happens when you run this program? What happens if you do press a key?

Try changing the number in line 25 to

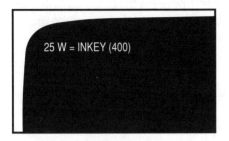

```
25 W = INKEY (400)
```

What happens?

If *you* want to control which LEDs are switched on, you must be able to change the variable. You can do this in the same way that you changed the co-ordinates in the drawing programs.

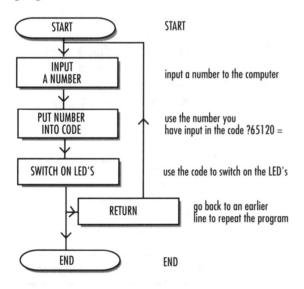

START — START

INPUT A NUMBER — input a number to the computer

PUT NUMBER INTO CODE — use the number you have input in the code ?65120 =

SWITCH ON LED'S — use the code to switch on the LED's

RETURN — go back to an earlier line to repeat the program

END — END

This gives us a program

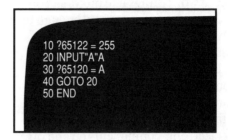

```
10 ?65122 = 255
20 INPUT"A"A
30 ?65120 = A
40 GOTO 20
50 END
```

Try to see if it works.

The computer will ask you for the number

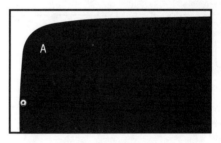

A

When you type in a number between 0 and 255 it will switch on the correct LEDs.

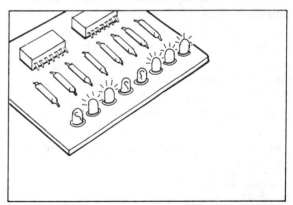

Project 19

Work out a flow chart and a program to light up each LED for three seconds in the order PB0 to PB7. **Hint:** A = A ★ 2 will multiply a variable (A) by 2 each time the program goes through that line.

Interfaces

We need an interface because a computer has not the power to work things like motors. You have just made an interface powerful enough to switch LEDs on and off. You will have to modify it to make it able to drive a larger component, like a motor. Integrated circuits, such as the ones you have used and the ones inside the computer, have a limited amount of power. But they do have enough power to switch other electronic components on and off. So we can link them to these components and let them do the hard work.

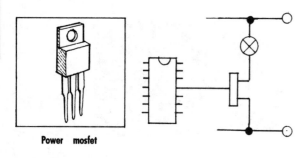

Power mosfet

There are some very new components, called **power mosfets**, which can do the job very easily. They are just like a **transistor**, so your teacher should be able to show you how to connect them to the interface. They are able to pass large amounts of current, and they can be controlled directly from the output of an integrated circuit. But because they are new, you may not have them in your school yet. If you do have them, they are the simplest way to do the job.

Transistor

Symbol for transistor

It is much more likely that you will have to use the electronic components that are available. So we will look in more detail at how to make the interface more powerful by using transistors and **relays**.

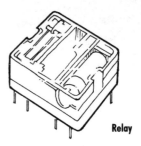

Relay

The relay is going to be the component that will do the main job. It is an electromechanical switch. It has mechanical contacts, the bits that come together to allow the electricity to flow, which are operated electrically; that is, they need an electric current to make them work. We will use a transistor to send this current to the relay, and hence work the contacts.

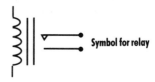

Symbol for relay

So the pieces will go together like this:

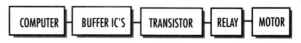

| COMPUTER | BUFFER IC'S | TRANSISTOR | RELAY | MOTOR |

It looks like a lot of messing about, but it really is the best way to get the computer to do what we want – to control motors.

Each of the eight output lines can have a transistor and relay connected to it. The new circuit is quite simple. First remove the LEDs.

The transistors are going to be connected in their place. Your teacher will explain in more detail, but a transistor has three connecting legs:

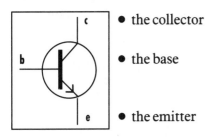

- the collector

- the base

- the emitter

The base lead must be connected to the resistor in the interface. The emitter lead goes to the 0v connection. The collector is then joined to the relay. A **diode** must also be joined to the collector to protect the transistor when the relay is switched on and off. The other side of both the relay and the diode are joined to the +v in the circuit (the positive side of the battery).

So each line from the buffers will have:

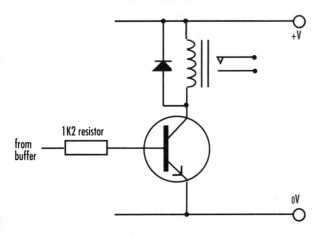

The components that you will need for each of the output lines are:
- BFY 51 transistor
- 9V relay
- 4001 diode

Note: The relay will have a lot of connections. Ask your teacher which ones to use.

Now, a motor with its own battery power supply can be joined to the mechanical contacts on the other side of the relay.

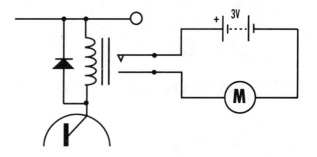

When the output line is switched on by the computer, the buffer turns on the transistor, which turns on the relay, which switches on the motor!

Project 20

Try connecting one line of the interface to a motor. Then write a program that will switch it on and off. Now use the $W = INKEY(\ \ )$ command to control how long the motor runs.

Fact File

- Present-day computers are not brains – they cannot think. But thinking computers are coming. In the early 1980s a specially programmed computer was left running constantly. Three years later it had discovered a new method for designing electronic circuits. It had also decided that it was a person, and not a computer!

Project 21

Now that you have an interface that can control motors, why not make something for it to control? Try designing and building a small vehicle. It must use two motors, each powered by batteries. It must also be small enough to fit on to this book.

Here are some of the things you should be thinking about when you are designing this vehicle:
- What shape should the chassis be?
- How many wheels should it have?
- How will it be steered?
- What construction and materials will be used?
- Where will the batteries and interface go?

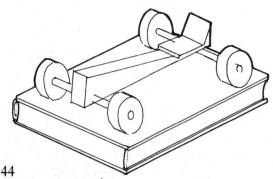

The next step is to write a program that will allow you to control the movement of the vehicle.

You might also like to design a body shell for the vehicle. Perhaps this could be vacuum formed. How about a logo and a colour scheme for the vehicle?

Once you have finished designing and making the vehicle, write a short report on how your vehicle and control program worked. Try to explain what were the good features and also what went wrong. Now make a list of improvements that you would include in your designs if you were to make the vehicle again.

You should by now have been able to write a program that allowed you to have a great deal of control over your vehicle. But there is one problem that you might have come across. You will probably have found that you can only get the motors to run in one direction. It would make control a lot easier if you could make the motors run backwards as well as forwards. The interface has eight output lines, so we could run eight motors in one direction. But by using two lines for each motor, it is possible to control four motors in both directions.

If a motor is connected to a battery, it will spin one way.

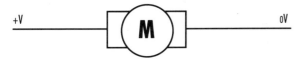

If the leads are connected the other way, the motor will spin the other way.

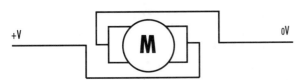

The relays contain a type of switch that allows the centre connection to join to one of two side connections. These are 'single pole double throw' switches.

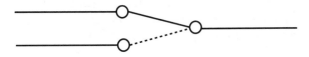

By some clever wiring, the two relays can be used to supply power to a motor in either direction.

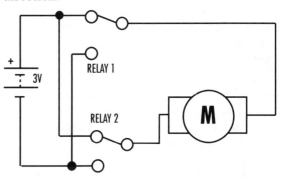

If both relays are off, the motor does not run.
If both relays are on, the motor does not run.
If relay 1 is on, and relay 2 is off, the motor will run in one direction.
If relay 1 is off, and relay 2 on, the motor will run in the other direction.

So once again, by careful control of the output lines, the computer can be used to control external devices.

Commercial Interfaces

There are many companies who will sell you an interface to save you the trouble of making your own. They all do slightly different things, and work using different methods. Some are better at their jobs than others and these can be a lot easier to use. Probably their main advantage is that they come with their own **software** (their own programs, which will probably be on a disc). This allows you to use the interface without having to worry about complicated programming. Instead they use a simplified version that works out all of the output codes for you.

The interface that we have chosen to look at is the Microelectronics Education Program (MEP) – Control It system. This comes in several versions, each with its own advantages. Some versions allow you to input information to the computer, but we will look at the system just as an output interface.

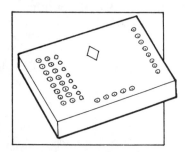

The Control It box works in a very similar way to the interface you have built. It has integrated circuits to act as buffers, and these are used to switch on/off transistors.

The box plugs into one (or on some versions, two) of the ports underneath the computer. It is supplied with power from batteries or a power pack. This power supply plugs into sockets on the top of the box.

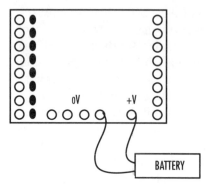

There is one socket for +v and several sockets for 0v. This is so that the 0v can be connected to the devices that you want to control.

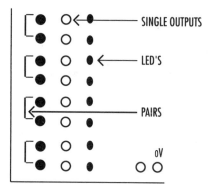

This would allow you to control bulbs, or you could control a motor (in one direction). To get forwards and reverse, the interface box uses the output lines in pairs, just as we did. The advantage is that connections are already made for you inside the box. So you only have to plug your motor into one of the pairs of sockets. Again, power for both the box and the motors is supplied by a battery connected to the power sockets.

Finally, there is a row of LEDs that allow you to see which of the output lines is switched on.

The connections for joining the interface box to the computer and to its output devices are quite simple. If you are unsure about them, ask your teacher. So we will look in more detail at the software that comes with the box. Obviously the manual will give you all of the details, but we will explain the commands you are likely to find most useful.

The Control It software disc has an **autoboot**. So put the disc into the drive and then hold down the SHIFT key and at the same time press the BREAK key. The program will automatically load from disc to the computer. The screen will show a lot of information, much of which we can ignore for now. The two main things we need to watch are whether the outputs are on or off, and if the clock is running.

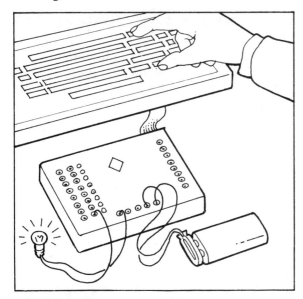

Let's use the box.

First plug the interface into the computer. Now autoboot the software disc. Finally, give the interface box some power by plugging in some batteries.

Single outputs are easy to control. Plug a bulb or buzzer into output 0. Remember, the 0v side is plugged into one of the 0v sockets on the box. To switch it on, type in:

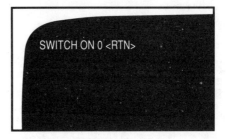

SWITCH ON 0 <RTN>

To switch it off, type in:

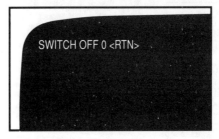

SWITCH OFF 0 <RTN>

Try this with some of the other outputs, and with some other devices.

We can build these commands into programs. So type in:

BUILD FRED <RTN>

Commercial Interfaces

This puts the software into the programming mode, and it is waiting for us to build a program called FRED. We can use the clock to keep the bulb on for a few seconds before we turn it off. So let's try a program.

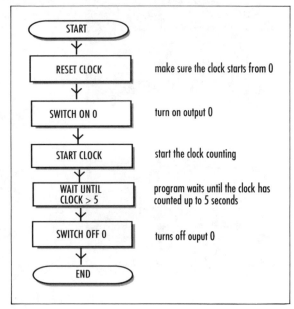

The flow chart looks good.

Now let's type in the program.

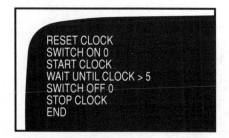

Now press the escape key to get out of the programming mode. To run the program simply type:

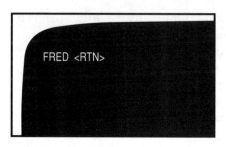

Did it work?

Yes – well done!

- Computers cannot make mistakes. The answers will always be correct if the program and the information given to the computer is correct. The errors are made by the people who operate the computers.

Project 22

Earlier we used our own program to control windows on the screen to make them into traffic-lights. Try changing this program so that you are now controlling bulbs using the Control It box.

What about motors?

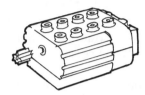

We have already said that the motors are plugged into pairs of output sockets. These pairs are labelled a,b,c,d. Plug a motor into the pair of sockets labelled a. You can get the motor to spin in two directions. Type in:

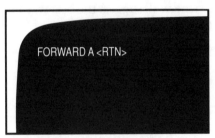

```
FORWARD A <RTN>
```

The motor should start spinning. Now type in:

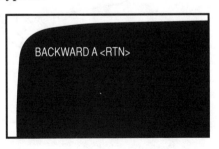

```
BACKWARD A <RTN>
```

The motor should spin in the other direction. To stop the motor, type in:

```
HALT A <RTN>
```

You can control more than one motor with the same command, such as FORWARD A,D. This can make a program much shorter.

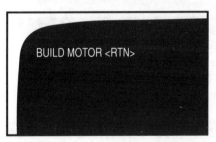

```
BUILD MOTOR <RTN>
```

There is one more trick that this interface has. It can alter the speed of the motor. Obviously the command we will use is SPEED, followed by a number: 1 is the slowest speed, 9 is the fastest. So with a motor connected to output sockets, pair a, let's try this program.

```
RESET CLOCK
SPEED 1
FORWARD A
START CLOCK
WAIT UNTIL CLOCK > 5
HALT A
WAIT UNTIL CLOCK > 7
SPEED 9
BACKWARD A
WAIT UNTIL CLOCK > 12
HALT A
STOP CLOCK
END
```

Escape from the programming mode and try out the program by typing:

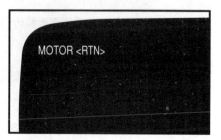

MOTOR <RTN>

Does it work as you had expected it to? Write down what each command did during the program.

Project 23

Connect your vehicle from Project 21 to this interface. Draw a route on the floor with some chalk. See if you can control your vehicle so that it follows the chalk line.

Project 24

For this project, design and make a **Scara**. Scara stands for Semi-Compliant Articulated Robot Arm.

That is a robot arm that has a limited number of movements. It will have two or three hinged joints, and may be able to pick up small objects. Most industrial robots are Scaras.

Set about the project in this order.
1 Find out as much as you can about Scaras: where they are used, what they are used for, how many movements they have, etc.
2 Decide what you want your Scara to do.
3 List the movements you will need. How many joints and motors will you need?
4 Sketch some designs for your Scara.
5 Model your Scara with a technical modelling kit, such as Lego Technic or Fischertechnik.

6 Test your model by writing a suitable control program. Then write a report that explains how your Scara may be improved.
7 Construct the final Scara. Some materials that may be of use are:
● art straws
● Corriflute
● Plawco

as well as the common workshop materials, such as:
● metals
● plastics
● timbers

Your teacher will suggest the best way of using these materials.

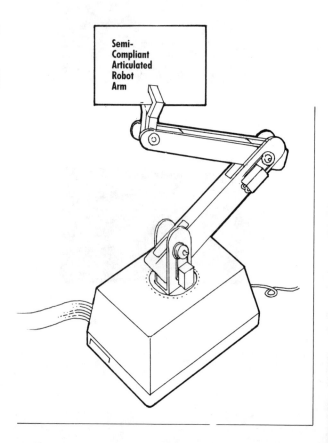

Semi-
Compliant
Articulated
Robot
Arm

Industrial Control

So far you have used the computer to control motors, LEDs, vehicles and robot arms. As you may already know, the principles you have used have become increasingly important to industry. You may have seen advertisements on TV for cars which are built by robots.

Computer control is used by industry in many different ways, for example:
- Car manufacture
- Electronics
- Bottle filling
- Filing
- Military purposes

Because of this, schools are starting to use CNC (computer numerically controlled) machines, such as lathes or milling machines. These work in basically the same way as industrial machines but are smaller and less powerful.

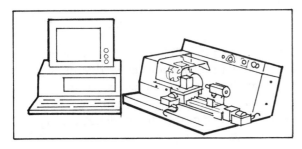

With schools having these machines, you can learn the principles of industrial CNC work.

A CNC machine works in basically the same way as a normal machine, the main difference being that instead of you controlling the machine directly, you program a computer which sends the information, via an interface, to motors on the machine.

This means that the computer can be used to repeat routines, as mentioned in earlier chapters, so that a CNC machine can make a large number of identical items. This is called batch production.

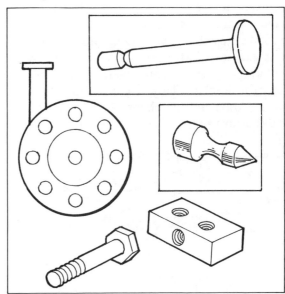

Items made on batch production include:
- parts for cars
- nuts and bolts
- furniture fittings
- valves
- pumps

Project 25

List as many things as you can that have been made on a CNC machine.

Fact File

- The average size of item made on a lathe in industry is less than 150 mm long and less than 50 mm diameter.

Technology and Computer Control

We have spent a lot of time looking at how to get the computer to control things – the screen, bulbs, motors, etc. But how does this fit into what you study at school?

First we must decide what **technology** is. The first stage is to find and look at a problem. Then we have to try and design something that can solve the problem. To get the best solution, you (as the designer) must choose the best materials and the most appropriate technology for the job.

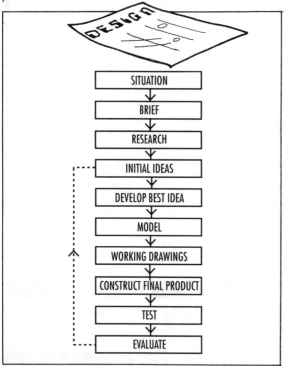

Over the last few years, computers have become much more powerful and very much cheaper. Their ability to control things makes them ideal for solving many of the problems that we are given as technology design briefs. On the next few pages you will find several design problems. Although some may seem difficult at first, the information you need to design a solution is contained in this book.

You may also want to try more complex computer control. Being able to input information to the computer helps a lot. So it is well worth reading more about this in the manuals that come with the interface devices.

Finally, remember that to solve any problem you should use all of your knowledge and skill to design the best solution, using the most appropriate technology, which may be materials, mechanisms, tools, electronics or computers.

Here is an example of how you might work through a technology project.

The *situation* is: a children's hospital needs a toy that will keep the young patients amused.

From this situation we could write a *design brief*:

Design and make a toy that includes lots of interesting features, which will be kept on a table in a children's hospital ward to amuse the patients.

Before starting to design a project, it is necessary to find out as much relevant information as you can. This is the *research*. You will have to find the answers to questions like:
- What will interest small children?
- What colours could be used?
- What materials can be used?
- How can I make sure that it is safe?
- How can movement be included?
- How can the movements be controlled?
- How big can it be?
- What other features could be included?

You should put your answers down as written notes and drawings to help you with your *initial ideas*. The ideas will be sketches of your designs with lots of notes to explain the details that cannot be seen.

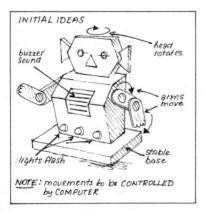

When you have chosen your best idea you need to add all of the details. This is when you develop the best idea.

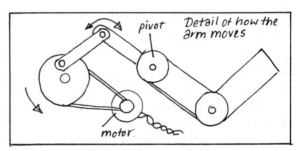

Next, you may need to *model* all of the working parts to check that the idea will work. You will also need to *develop* the computer program to control the features.

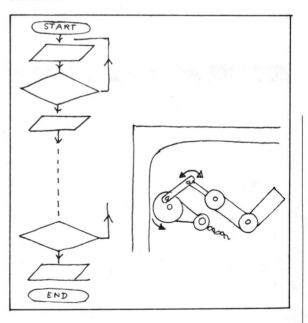

Technology and Computer Control

If everything works, then it is time to produce accurate *working drawings* of all the parts that will have to be made.

You can use them to *construct the final product*.

Once everything is finished, *test* the toy to see if it does the job described in the brief. This may mean taking it to the hospital to try it out. If it works well you can write a good *evaluation*, but you may have come across some problems, which should also be explained in the evaluation. You will then have to go back to your initial ideas to try to put them right.

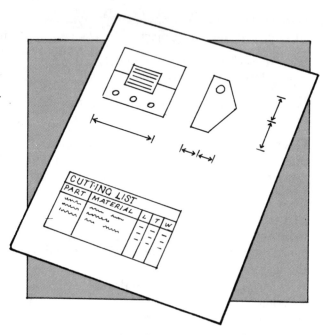

Project 35

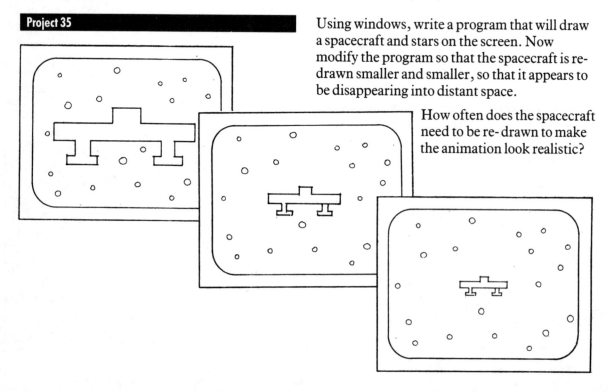

Using windows, write a program that will draw a spacecraft and stars on the screen. Now modify the program so that the spacecraft is re-drawn smaller and smaller, so that it appears to be disappearing into distant space.

How often does the spacecraft need to be re-drawn to make the animation look realistic?

Project 26

Use the MOVE and DRAW commands to design a logo with your initials. If your school has a suitable DUMP routine (ask your teacher about this), print out your logo to use on the cover of your note book.

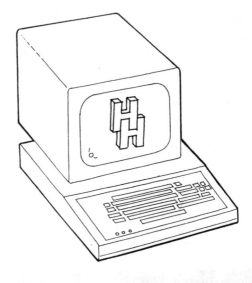

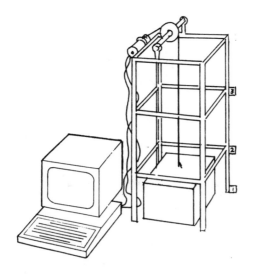

Project 27

Design and build a lift that can be stopped at different levels. Now program the computer so that you can press a key to choose which level the lift will stop at.

Project 28

Design a program that uses graphics windows to test your speed of reaction. *Hint*: windows could be coloured in at timed intervals until you press a key.

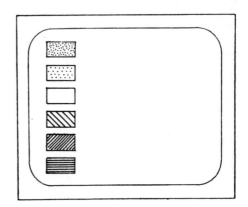

Technology and Computer Control

Project 29: An Anti-Burglar Device

Construct a scale model of a room. Use the information in this book to write a program which will control, through an interface, the lights and the curtains to make it appear that somebody is at home.

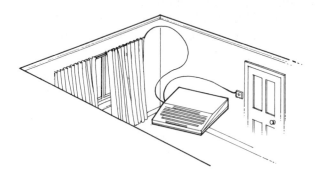

Project 30: Games

Using the information on screen control, design a game, such as Noughts and Crosses or Battleships. Areas of the screen are coloured in using VDU and GCOL commands. The final game could be adapted to play against the computer. *Hint:* RND.

Project 31: Remote Control

Use the information in the control sections to combine screen and external control. Now write a program which will control a vehicle. As the vehicle moves, its path should be shown on the screen.

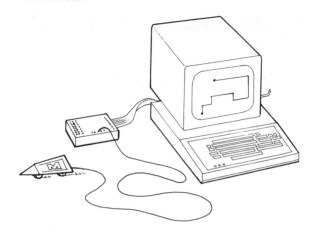

Project 32: Timer

Write a program which will allow a friend to choose one item from a list of household appliances, such as cooker, TV, radio. When the choice has been made, he or she should be able to turn the appliance on, leave it on for a certain time, and then turn it off again. Each appliance could be represented either by a window on the screen or by simple devices attached through an interface.

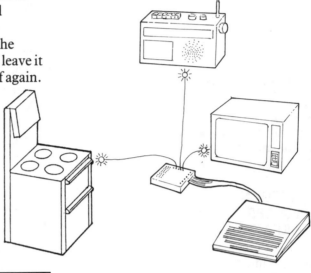

Project 33: Bounce

Write a program to produce the effect of a bouncing ball on the screen.

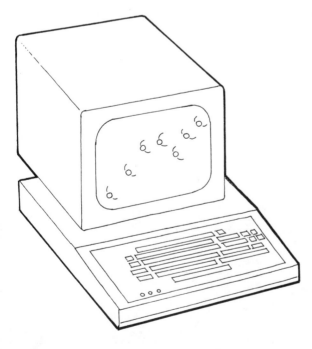

Project 34: Scara

A shopkeeper wants a display in his window to show the 'great versatility' of Scaras. Design a program which will be suitable for his display.

Revision

Here are a few questions that you can use to see how well you have remembered what is in this book.

1 What is a computer?
2 Make a list of five devices that use a computer.
3 What are the five parts of a computer, and what do they do?
4 There is a sixth part associated with a computer, the backing store. What is the most common type of backing store?
5 What do the following keys on the keyboard do?

     RETURN
     ESCAPE
     BREAK

6 How does the computer know that you are typing in a line to a program rather than just a command?
7 What command does the computer need before it will carry out the instructions in a program?
8 What is a flow chart? Why is it useful?
9 What is the VDU command to draw a graphics window?
10 How can you change the colour of the window?
11 How can you make the window visible on the screen?
12 What does the command W=INKEY(200) do?
13 List four commands associated with the disc-drive.
14 What is the difference between the MOVE and DRAW commands?
15 What is the VDU command for a text window? How do the co-ordinates differ from those used with graphics windows?
16 What is a port on a computer?
17 How do you tell the computer to switch on the user port?
18 To tell the computer to turn on lines in the user port the code ?65120= is used along with a binary number. How is the number worked out?
19 What is the purpose of the interface?
20 What does the command RND(100) do?
21 Why can't a motor be driven by an integrated circuit?
22 What component is used to turn the motor on/off?
23 What type of switch can be used to help you control the direction the motor runs?
24 Why is it sometimes simpler to use a commercial interface?
25 What is a Scara?
26 List five places where a Scara might be used.

Mini-Dictionary

Autoboot A means of loading a program from disc and running it in one operation.

BASIC This is a special language for the computer. We understand English; the computer understands BASIC.

Batch Computer-controlled machines are best at making large numbers of one product at any one time. So the machine is set up to produce a batch of parts – batch production.

Binary A counting system made up from just the numbers 0 and 1. Ideally suited for computers as they run on electricity which can be on or off: 0 is represented by off, 1 is represented by on.

Break One of the keys on the BBC computer keyboard. If it is pressed, the computer stops what it is doing. Normally, if it is pressed, the program the computer was running will be lost.

Buffer A computer is a delicate electronic device. It can easily be damaged, so it must be protected from stray voltages from the things it is controlling. An integrated circuit is used as a buffer to protect the computer.

CAD Computer-aided design. One of the most time-consuming parts of design is the drawing. Each time a part is modified, new drawings have to be made. Computers are now used to aid the designer by speeding up the drawing processes.

CLG A command in BASIC which clears the graphics window of any drawings. It can also be used to make the window visible on the screen.

CLS A command in BASIC which clears all of the VDU screen. It can be used at the beginning of a program to remove text, etc. Useful if you want a clear screen so that you see only what the program has done.

CNC Computer numerically controlled. Describes machines that are controlled by computers.

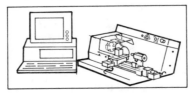

Co-ordinate A pair of numbers used to locate a point. Co-ordinates are used for graphs and maps, as well as for finding points in a computer window.

CPU Central Processor Unit. This is the electronic heart of the computer, where all the information given to the computer is processed.

Decimal A counting system using base 10. It is the system that we usually use.

Device Something that does a job can be called a device. So a computer could be a device, as could an electric motor.

Dry run A dry run is like a test run. Before writing the final program, you can try it out in your head or on paper. That way you should spot any problems early and be able to put them right before typing them into the computer.

Electronic Electronic components are the parts that make things like computers work. They can be switched on and off by electricity, or they can control where the electricity goes and what it does.

Element Element is another name for part. An element of a system is a part of a system.

Escape A key on the BBC computer. If you press the escape key when a program is running, the program will stop. Hopefully the program will not be lost. In the Control It software, the key is also used to escape from the programming mode, so that the program can then be run.

Flow chart A method of organizing your thoughts when writing a computer program. Each command or operation that you want the computer to do is put into a box. The boxes are put into order with arrows showing the flow through the program.

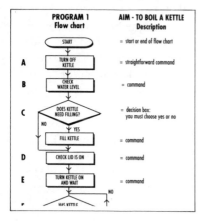

Format Formatting is the process of preparing a disc for use. It puts into place the tracks on which the information will be stored. A disc is useless until it has been formatted.

GOTO A command in BASIC. When the program reaches this command, the computer goes to the line number given after the GOTO command.

INPUT A lot of programs need extra information from the keyboard while they are running. This command in BASIC tells the computer to wait for some information to be input.

Integrated circuit Also known as an IC or microchip. It is a small plastic package which contains a large number of miniaturized electronic components. These have been set up as complete electronic circuits. Connections to the

circuit are made through the metal legs in the sides of the plastic package.

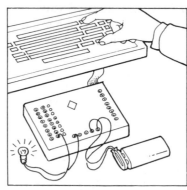

Interface A device made up from electronic and electromechanical components. It goes between the computer and the device that the computer is controlling. It provides the power for the external device, and also protects the computer from damage. Some interfaces can be used to input information to the computer.

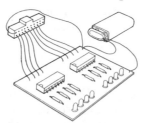

Language If you typed a program into the computer in English, it wouldn't understand it. It needs its own language, with its own words and commands and punctuation. There are lot of computer languages. The

BBC computer understands BASIC.

Logo This is a special type of sign or symbol that is used to represent a company or its products, etc. A logo will allow you to recognize the company without seeing the name.

Microchip *See* Integrated circuit.

Mode The computer has different ways of working, which are called modes. Some are used when the computer is working with text. Some are used when the computer is working with graphics or pictures.

Peripheral Lots of things can be attached, or plugged in, to the computer. These are called the peripherals. Among them are the VDU, the disc-drive, the printer and the interface.

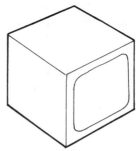

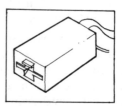

Ports The sockets in the computer where the peripherals are plugged in. Most of the ports are underneath the computer.

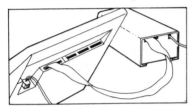

Program A list of instructions for the computer. It is used to tell the computer what you want it to do. A program will contain a lot of commands. Each line of commands is given a number. It is important that these commands are in the correct order.

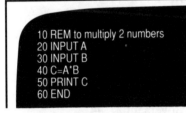

```
10 REM to multiply 2 numbers
20 INPUT A
30 INPUT B
40 C=A*B
50 PRINT C
60 END
```

Relay A switch that can be turned on and off by an electric current. Relays are useful as switches in interfaces.

Return A key on the BBC computer. It tells the computer when you have finished typing a command or a line of a program. So the return key is used a lot.

RND A special command for the computer. It tells the computer to think up a number at random. It is useful if you want the computer to try things for itself, or if you want to play against the computer.

RUN This is the command that starts a program working. You type in RUN and then press the return key. The computer will then start running through your list of instructions.

Scara A name given to some robot arms. They have a limited amount of movement, with normally only two or three hinge joints. A computer is used to control the motors that move the joints.

Technology The use of materials, mechanisms, electronics, control systems, etc., to solve design problems.

Transistor An electronic component. It normally has three wire legs that are connected to the rest of the circuit. It can be used as a switch inside devices like the interface.

Turtle The small buggies that can be controlled by a computer. They got their name because the domed plastic cover that protects their workings looks a bit like a turtle's shell.

Variable Many programs need numbers to tell the computer what to do, for instance, where to draw the next line. You need to be able to change some numbers, like co-ordinates of a point, so these numbers are called variables. In a program, the computer is told to expect a variable number when a command has given a letter as a label.

VDU The visual display unit is the screen on which you see what the computer is doing.

Window An area on the screen. A window can be used to show drawings on the screen. You can also have windows that keep the text in one part of the screen.

Index

Abacus 5
ACCESS 26
Arithmetic unit 8
Art straws 50
Autoboot 47

Background 22, 29
Backing store 8, 25
BACKWARD 49
Base 43
BASIC 10, 15
Batch 51
Battery 37, 46
BBC Master 7, 10, 34
BBC Model B 7, 10, 34
BBC Model B+ 7, 10, 34
Binary 6, 35, 36
Break 10, 16
Buffer 37, 38, 42, 46
Buggies 34
BUILD 47, 49
Bulb 37, 47
Buzzer 47

Calculations 5, 19
Caps lock 13
Cassette player 11, 13
Cassettes 8
Catalogue 25, 26
Central processor 8, 11, 12
Chassis 44
Circuit diagram 39
CLG 22
Clock 48, 49
CLS 14
CNC 51
Co-ordinates 21, 32, 33
Codes 21, 33, 36
Collector 43
Colossus 6
Colour 21, 29
Columns 35
Commands 17, 25
Commercial 46

Components 37, 39
Computer 5, 14, 37
Construction 50
Contacts 42
Control 6, 20, 37, 40, 52
Control It 46
Control Unit 8
Corriflute 50
CPU 8, 11, 14
Current 42
Cursor 10

Decimal 35
DEF PROC 18
Design 50, 52
Diode 43
DRAW 27, 28, 30, 31
Disc-drive 11, 12, 13, 25
Dry run 17, 19

Electronic 8, 37
Element 9
Emitter 43
END 16, 18
Escape 10, 16, 40
External 34, 37, 40

File 25
Floppy discs 8, 25, 47
Flow chart 17, 30, 47
Foreground 22, 29
Format 25
FORWARD 49

GCOL 22, 24, 27
GOTO 16, 31, 40
Graphics 20, 33
Graphs 20

HALT 49

IC 4050 39
IF THEN 18
Industry 51

Information 8, 9, 12, 14
INKEY 24, 40
INPUT 8, 9, 30, 31
Instructions 15, 17, 20
Integrated circuit 37, 39
Interfaces 37, 38, 42, 44, 46

Key 10
Keyboard 8, 10, 12, 14

Language 15
Lathe 51
LED 39, 40, 46
Line 15, 16, 36, 38
Line number 15
LIST 16
LOAD 25, 26
Logo 44
Loop 16, 30

Mains voltage 13
Memory 12, 16
MEP 46
Microchip 37
Milling machine 51
Modes 22, 29
Motor 37, 42, 45, 49
MOVE 28, 30, 31
Movement 27, 44

Output 8, 34, 46
Output lines 36, 43

Peripheral 11
Pictures 20
Plawco 50
Ports 11, 34
Power mosfet 42
PRINT 15, 16, 19, 25
Printer 11, 13
PROC 18
Program 15, 22
Programming 15, 27, 30, 46

Random 40
Relay 42, 43, 45, 46
REM 18, 19
REPEAT UNTIL 18
Resistor 38, 39
Return 10, 14
RND 40
Robot 12, 50, 51
RUN 15, 16, 19

SAVE 25, 33
Scara 50
Screen 8, 13, 22

Shift-break 47
Software 46
Storage unit 8
Switch 42, 48
Symbol 42

Techniques 17
Text 20
Tracks 25
Transformer 37
Transistor 42, 43, 46
Turtle 34

User port 34

Vacuum formed 44
Variable 19, 40
VDU 8, 11, 12, 13, 14, 20, 21,
   27, 33
Vehicle 44

WAIT 48, 49
WIPE 26
Window 20, 22, 33
Word processor 33